# THE GOOD MAN CHALLENGE

## A 30-DAY DEVOTIONAL FOR MEN

# KEITH MARTIN

# Table of Contents

" **God has given every man the opportunity to be a leader!**

**-Keith Martin**

*First published by Revival Publishing 2021 Copyright © 2021 by Keith Martin*

*First edition*

# FOREWORD

\* \* \*

Society often talks about what defines a **good man**. Ask any given person what makes a man **good,** and we would receive a variety of answers on any given day. This book challenges the **good** character of men, which is rooted in godly and biblical principles. **The GOOD MAN Challenge** is the perfect, practical guide for helping **men** strengthen their relationship with God, strengthen their relationship with others, and boost their growth in God.

The author strives to be a **good man** in every aspect of his life. For over 18 years, I have watched this **good man** evolve into who he is today. I see this **good man's** public side, and I see this **good man's** private side; what you are receiving from this book is coming from a genuine place.

There is nothing to lose with the purchase of this book, only an investment in your benefits and gains. A **good man** will benefit and gain in his relationship with God, in his relationship with his spouse, in his relationship with his children, in his relationship with his family, in his relationships with his friends, and within his relationships in this world.

Sharon D. Hamilton-Martin

# DEDICATION

\* \* \*

## I would like to dedicate this book to:

**First, this book is dedicated to and devoted to Jesus Christ:** He is truly the Lord and Savior of my life!

**My wife, Sharon:** She pushed me to write this book. She makes my life better!

**My boys, Solomon and Zechariah:** I love being their dad!

**My late Grandfather, Pastor John R. Gaudy:** The greatest man I have known. My hero!

**My Grandmother Florine:** The Queen of Wisdom

**My Mother, Valerie:** Prayer Warrior and Anointed Vessel

**My late Father: Keith Martin, Sr.:** Who was loved by many.

**My late Stepfather "Pops," Elder Columbus Sykes:** He showed me the meaning of hard work.

**My Siblings: Kendra, Valente' Antoine, Vinson, and Aaron.** I love you all!

**Pastors who lead the flock:** Keep leading the congregation and stay anointed!

**The Saints!** They help to make me who I am. I love God's people.

**The Men of God who influenced my life:** Thank you for pouring into me!

# INTRODUCTION

\* \* \*

## The steps of a good man are ordered by the LORD: and he delighteth in his way. (Psalms 37:23)

**How do you define a GOOD MAN? What does he look like?**

**What are his attributes? Are there any Good Men?**

**How do I become a Good Man?**

When women are asked what makes a GOOD MAN, most will answer:

1.  He is Attractive
2.  He is Driven
3.  He is Financially Stable
4.  He is a Protector
5.  He is a Good Father
6.  He is Sensitive
7.  He is a Good Lover

Depending on the woman, she may have her GOOD MAN list. If you ask men the same question, they will probably have a similar plan with different priorities. Most men worldwide experience the daily pressures of being a man but may not know how to answer the question: "What is a GOOD MAN?"

The good news is that God has something to say about this. The Bible declares that "*The steps of a GOOD MAN are ordered by the LORD: and he delighteth in his way.*" *(Psalms 37:23)*. In this text, the "Good Man's" steps are guided or directed by God's leading. The original Hebrew word for **man** in this text is *gabar* גבר *(gaw- bar')* which means **"mighty man"** or **"warrior."** This Word is gender-specific (not gender-neutral), this scripture is talking about a warrior who is male. (Sorry, ladies). The Bible says a man that the Lord leads is a **mighty warrior** in God's eyes. The

**7**

Lord is pleased by a man that allows Him to lead and guide his life's journey! The Word of God has given the roadmap for every man to become a GOOD MAN.

I'm a husband, father, minister, and pastor. I also still work for a living. All of my responsibilities can be overwhelming at times. Most men understand that there are unique pressures that come with being a man. Although expectations can be put on us by others, the most challenging expectations sometimes come from ourselves. We don't have all the answers, and when we don't have the answers, that is where faith, prayer, and studying the Word of God come in. I have over twenty (20) years of ministry experience. One of the biggest obstacles I have encountered in these years was finding an easy reading devotional that addresses every man's unique pressures in this life. As a result, the Lord led me to write this book. I pray that this book is a blessing to men all over the world.

This book gives thirty (30) days of challenges designed for the reader to become the GOOD MAN described in **Psalms 37:23**. Trust the process. Men worldwide will take this journey with you. I'm taking this journey with you myself. It does not matter where you are in your faith in God; these challenges are for your spiritual and faith growth. Keep an open mind, heart, and spirit. Use this resource in Sunday School, men's group, small groups, youth groups, prison bible study, personal devotion, etc. Fathers, father-figures, mentors, grandfathers, uncles, preachers, pastors, and all men who want to grow in the faith will benefit from these challenges.

While there are 30 days of challenges, every man taking this journey has a "hands-on" part to play in his development. Don't worry about anyone judging you; you are doing this for yourself! God will do His part; we have to do our part to grow and go forward. You can do this! Your family, your community, and you will be better because you are taking this journey. Decide today to be a better man, a GOOD MAN.

**Before we start, pray this prayer aloud:**

Father, I have decided to become a better man, the GOOD MAN you called me to be. Open my mind, heart, and spirit so that I can receive everything you want to give me to go forward and grow. Lord, I need your help, and I want YOU to help me.

Help me Lord, in Jesus' name,

AMEN!

Now, turn the page, and let's start this journey.

# DAY 1 | THE STARTING POINT

\* \* \*

**"The steps of a good man are ordered by the LORD, And He delights in his way. Though he falls, he shall not be utterly cast down; For the LORD upholds him with His hand."**
**(Psalms 37:23-24 NKJV)**

## ARE. YOU. READY?

The original Hebrew word for man in this text is **gabar גֶּבֶר (gaw-bar')** which means **"mighty man"** or **"warrior."** In the text in the NASB (New American Standard Bible), we see the word "established." This word "established" was translated from the original text כּוּן **or kun (koon),** which means *"to be firm, order, or to be appointed."* We should desire to be a "mighty man" or a "warrior" in the Lord. To be what God called us to be, we have to let God "establish" or "appoint" the steps of our life journey.

Sometimes in this life, feeling like a "mighty" man can be a challenge itself. The pressures that we face as men can seem overwhelming at times. We are under pressure almost ALL THE TIME. We have pressure to perform in the classroom, on the job, and sometimes even in the church. The more people depend on us, the more pressure we have. Brothers, I'm going to present you with this truth: YOU CAN'T DO THIS ON YOUR OWN. We need the Lord to "order our steps" because most of us have tried to navigate life, but we realize we need help from God. The purpose of this challenge is to allow the Lord to guide our life. As men, we are used to being in control. Or, we are used to feeling like we are in control of what is around us. Brothers, let us allow God to have full control of our steps.

# THE CHALLENGE

Allow God to be your guide from today forward. It starts with Jesus being your Savior and Lord. The beginning of a godly and guided life begins with us accepting Jesus Christ in our hearts and recognizing that we need the Lord to lead us every day. If you never committed your life to Jesus, I challenge you to do that right now. My brother, if you have not already given your life to Jesus, I challenge you to do it now, from the bottom of your heart. A simple, sincere prayer of repentance will get you on track. We need the Lord to be our guide!

## A Prayer of Repentance and Dedication

The Bible tells us in Romans 10:9 (NIV), "If you declare with your mouth, "Jesus is Lord," and believe in your heart that God raised him from the dead, you will be saved. For it is with your heart that you believe and is justified, and it is with your mouth that you profess your faith and are saved." **Verse 13** goes on to say, "*Whosoever calls on the name of the Lord shall be saved.*" "Whosoever" means you and me! For Repentance and Dedication, repeat this prayer out loud:

"Dear Jesus, I want you to guide my life. You said in Your Word that if I acknowledge that You were raised from the dead and that I accept you as my Lord and Savior, that I would be saved. So, God, I now say that I believe You are MY RISEN SAVIOR, and I want you now to be Lord over my life! I accept my salvation from sin right now.

Thank you, Father God, for forgiving me, saving me, and giving me eternal life with You. Now Lord, be my guide! I need your direction! I will follow you for the rest of my life! Amen!" If you wholeheartedly believe this prayer. Jesus is right now your LORD, SAVIOR, and GUIDE!

## DAY 2 | ESTABLISHED AND FIRM IN THE FAITH

\* \* \*

**The steps of a man are established by the LORD, And He delights in his way. (Psalms 37:23 KJV)**

**How did the first Challenge go?** Now we are allowing God to be our guide going forward. Let's continue, mighty warrior!

As a man, are you "firm" in your faith? Do you believe that God is on our side? Do you have a heart that wants to please God? Do you want a closer relationship with Jesus Christ? If the answer is Yes, you won half of the battle. The journey of a believer is a walk of faith! My brother, your FAITH, is going to be challenged. That's is why you need to allow God to continue to lead and guide your journey. As a Warrior in God's army, you have to get your orders. Your direct orders come from the Word of God. For the Word of God declares, **"...So then faith comes by hearing, and hearing by the Word of God." (Romans 10:17)** The Word of God builds your faith. The more you hear and study the Word, the more you become firm in the faith!

# *THE CHALLENGE*

Ask God to "*establish*" and "*appoint*" the direction that we take. We all have a purpose God is calling us to. We will not get there unless God "*establishes*" and "*appoint*" our steps. Whatever direction we were going, He will point us in the right direction if we ask. Know that your faith will be challenged! When your faith is challenged, be firm! Let this be the day that you decide that you will dedicate yourself to studying God's Word and hearing the Preached Word of God.

# DAY 3 | BEWARE OF WICKED COUNSEL

\* \* \*

**How blessed is the person who does not take the advice of the wicked, who does not stand on the path with sinners, and who does not sit in the seat of mockers? (Psalms 1:1 ISV)**

Brothers, we have to consider the sources where we are getting our counsel or advice. Who is influencing us? Are we getting our counsel, advice, or influence from Godly sources? Who or what do we look to for examples? We are all affected by something or someone. It is up to us as men to be cautious of who or what we allow to influence us!

The text used in this challenge from Psalms 1:1 expresses the blessing of not being influenced by the wicked or "ungodly" counsel. The word "counsel" is coming from the original Hebrew text of עֵצָה or etsah (ay-tsaw'), which means *"advice, consultation, plans, purpose, or strategy."* Our direction is often dictated by our sources of advice and who or what influences us. Evil counsel can destroy relationships, lead us in the wrong direction, and have many adverse effects on our lives! You don't have to walk alone because God can (and will) send someone in your life that will give you wise counsel. There are men of God in this world that are living for Him and are full of wisdom. Wise counsel is available if you ask God.

# *THE CHALLENGE*

Do a self-evaluation of who or what you are allowing to influence you. Do the things of God influence you? Are your results bringing you closer to the Lord or separating you from Him? Ask God to uproot every evil force in your life.

# DAY 4 | STANDING ON THE WRONG ROAD

\* \* \*

**How blessed is the person who does not take the advice of the wicked, who does not stand on the path with sinners, and who does not sit in the seat of mockers? (Psalms 1:1 ISV)**

As we continue from the Day 3 challenge, we will continue today with the New International Version of Psalms 1:1. In this translation of the text, we see the phrase "stand on the path with sinners." In the original Hebrew, the word for the path is **derek דְּרָכִים (deh'-rek)** which means way, path, roadway, or highway. This text lets us know that we are not blessed if we are going down the same path, walking the same way as "the sinner." Even deeper, the believer and the sinners should not be walking together going to the same destinations. Does this mean we don't talk or fellowship with "the sinner?" That point is heavily debated. The Word warns us of going in the same direction as the sinner if we confess that we have been born again. The Lord wants you to walk in the path of **eternal life, holiness, and righteousness!**

On what road will you stand? What highway will you travel on in life? What direction will you go? Every day we have to determine our path. Satan will always try to convince us to go in his direction, no matter how long we walk with God. Don't let Satan win! God has given us the tools to walk on the right path. Remember, **The Holy Spirit** is our **compass** *(the divine instrument pointing us in the right direction),* and the **Word of God** is our **roadmap** *(the detailed guide of the path to our destination).* On what road will you stand?

**14**

# *THE CHALLENGE*

Do a self-evaluation of who you are "walking" with. Will you continue to keep company with people with ungodly lifestyles? If so, why keep company with people who continue to live ungodly lifestyles? We must ask God to change our direction and our company.

# DAY 5 | SITTING IN THE WRONG SEAT

\* \* \*

## Blessed is the man that walketh not in the counsel of the ungodly, nor standeth in the way of sinners, nor sitteth in the seat of the scornful. (Psalms 1:1 KJV)

Today, we continue with Psalms 1:1. What does it mean to *"sitteth in the seat of the scornful"* as King James Version of the Bible reads? The New American Standard Bible says, *"sit in the seat of scoffers,"* and the New International Version says, *"sit in the company of mockers."* What is the Word trying to tell us, brothers? Let's take a more in-depth look at this text.

The original Hebrew reads וּבְמוֹשַׁב לֵצִים or **moshab (mo-shawb') luts (loots)**, this means the assembly of **disrespectful, spiteful, hateful, nasty, mean people** which is the opposite of what God wants us to be. Brothers, you cannot move forward being full of scorn (intense feelings of contempt, not showing respect for people, hateful, vindictive, always angry). Being scornful will destroy the meaningful relationships in your life. Brothers, we can't be scornful fathers, friends, sons, husbands, or leaders. Also, being scornful will hinder your spiritual walk. Brothers, why would you want to hinder your blessings or your walk with God because you keep company with "the scornful." Better yet, do you want to spend the rest of your life being scornful? You are better than that, man! My brother, let's get off the *"seat of the scornful!"*

**I pray, in the name of Jesus, that the chains of scornfulness be broken off of your life, forever!**

# *THE CHALLENGE*

Let's search our hearts. Are we disrespectful, spiteful, hateful, nasty, or mean? Do we show this behavior to our loved ones or coworkers? Does a person that shows this behavior have a significant influence on us? If so, let's ask God to forgive us and deliver us from these behaviors. We do not have to "sit on the seat of the scornful." Mighty warrior, change your seat!

# DAY 6 | BRAND NEW

\* \* \*

**Therefore, if anyone is in Christ, the new creation has come: The old has gone, the new is here! (2 Corinthians 5:17 NIV)**

We talked about the dangers of *"standing in the way of the sinner"* and *"sitting in the seat of the scornful."* What does it mean to be a believer? What does it mean to be "born again?" It is debated by many what being a Christian truly means. Let's see what the Word of God says about the matter, brothers.

The text above speaks of a "new creation." Being Saved, Born Again, Christian, a Believer, or any other phase to identify us with Christ means that a transformation has happened in our life. Every one of us who is indeed "saved" has repented (which means we asked God to forgive us of our sins and then turned away from that sinful life). We become the "new creation" mentioned in the above text after we are converted. We are now "in Christ!" We are in His grace, His love, His favor, His will, and His righteousness. There is now a DIFFERENCE in our sinful past life than our new "saved" life. We are now changed. We act differently, speak differently, think differently, treat others differently, etc. The world is confused about what it means to be a true believer because they can't see a difference between a person who is confessing to be "saved" and the person who lives a "worldly" life!

# *THE CHALLENGE*

Let our lives reflect the "new creation" that we have become. If you never genuinely repented of the sin in your life, you can do it now. Right now, you can ask Jesus to be your Lord and Savior. Ask Him to wash you of your sin. Ask Him to you make you a new creation. (See the Day 1 Challenge). Make a habit of repenting daily. Brothers, we are called to be a reflection of Jesus Christ. Let's be the believer God has called us to be.

# *DAY 7* | OUT WITH THE OLD

\* \* \*

**This means that anyone who belongs to Christ has become a new person. The old life is gone; a new life has begun! (2 Corinthians 5:17 NLT)**

*How is it going so far? We are a week into this journey! Congrats, my brother! Let's go even further:*

Let's look deeper at **2 Corinthians 5:17**, which leads me to ask this question: Brothers, is your "old life" truly gone? If not, why are you holding on to it? Salvation is about God making a person new. Brand new! Memorize this bible verse, "This means that anyone who belongs to Christ has become a new person. The old life is gone; a new life has begun!"

Jesus died for us that we may be new, transformed, changed by His power, not our own strength. When we accept Jesus Christ into our hearts, a transformation takes place in us. The old life is gone! Our old behaviors, mindset, habits, and methods that were displeasing to God should no longer be apart of our lives. The desire to do anything ungodly should be gone. Our lives are forever changed. So again, brothers, is our "old life" truly gone?

Does this mean we will not make mistakes? No, because in all likelihood, we will make mistakes. We will make some unwise decisions on this journey. Some of us may even fall on our face, both figuratively and literally. When you fall, don't stay down! Don't live in defeat. GET UP! Ask God to help you to get up and stay up! Whatever you do, don't go back to your old life!

For some, this is the struggle. Most of us want to do things our way. Our old self doesn't want to die. Some will say, "this is who I am." "This is who I will always be." **That is a lie; God can change you! He can change your heart and mind. You can be a new creation! Out with the OLD!**

# THE CHALLENGE

Let our life "old life" die today! Do you find yourself desiring things from your "old life?" Has a transformation indeed taken place in your life? If the answer is no, repent to God so that you can experience your "new life!"

## DAY 8 | CELEBRATING NEW LIFE!

\* \* \*

**This means that anyone who belongs to Christ has become a new person. The old life is gone; a new life has begun! (2 Corinthians 5:17 NLT)**

We are continuing on our journey, embracing our new life! Brothers, have you embraced the **new life**? Long time born-again believers, I have a question: **Do you still have joy?** Oh, the joy and peace that comes with salvation! The late, legendary gospel artist Walter Hawkins wrote a song called "Changed." One verse in the song says, *"He changed my life, and now I'm free!"* What are we free from? We are free from living a sinful life. We are free from being bound by sin. We are free from being used by Satan! **How powerful is that!** These are only some of the benefits of the **"new life"** in Christ. It is the most significant decision a person can make!

Joy and peace come with this divine inward change. This joy gives strength, *"for the joy of the Lord is your strength." (Nehemiah 8:10)* This change provides *"the peace of God, which surpasses all understanding, will guard your hearts and your minds in Christ Jesus." (Philippians 4:7)* Salvation comes with so many spiritual and natural benefits. You will experience these benefits as God continues to order your steps. Celebrate your new life! My brother, if you have been a born-again believer for a while, perform a **joy check**! Do you still enjoy being a born-again believer? If the answer is no, receive JOY right now! Receive the PEACE of God, now! Salvation has benefits! **Celebrate!**

# *THE CHALLENGE*

Take at least 5-10 minutes to celebrate your new life in Christ! Be thankful He saved you! No matter what is going on in your life now, give God praise NOW for your relationship with Him. Again, if you haven't experienced this change, do it now with a simple prayer of repentance. (See the Day 1 Challenge). Let's embrace and celebrate our NEW LIFE!

## DAY 9 | FINDING HELP

\* \* \*

*"I will lift up mine eyes unto the hills, from whence cometh my help. My help cometh from the Lord, which made heaven and earth." (Psalms 121:1-2 KJV)*

### HELP!

Brothers, we sometimes have trouble admitting that we need help from anyone. Some of us see it as a sign of weakness. Men do not like to be vulnerable. As husbands and fathers, our families depend on us. We want to show them that we are strong!

Where do we look to when we need help? The Psalms is letting us know that we can *"look to the hills."* The **help** is not in the hills but beyond. That is what the Psalm writer is expressing to us. Beyond the mountains, beyond the skies, and beyond anything we can see with our natural eye, there is divine help that we can look to. A GOOD MAN recognizes that our **"help"** truly comes from the Lord. His **"help"** is available for every area of our lives!

# THE CHALLENGE

Go to your Heavenly Father for help from this day forward! We don't have to depend on our own strength. You will find that your load will become lighter.

24

## DAY 10 | WE HAVE HELP

\* \* \*

### "God is our refuge and strength, A very present help in trouble." (Psalm 46:1)

Brothers, we have help! We do not have to face life's battles alone. The Word help comes from the Hebrew word or **ezer** עֵזֶר **(ay'-zer)**, which means **help** or **helper**. This is divine help that comes only from God. You can receive this help by seeking God for it! His divine **"help"** is available for every believer.

The Psalm writer is proclaiming the source of his real "*help.*" As believers, we understand the real source of our help comes from the Father. Jesus spoke of "*another comforter," "advocate," or "helper"* in the person of the Holy Spirit. "*But when the Father sends the Advocate as my representative—that is, the Holy Spirit—He will teach you everything and will remind you of everything I have told you.*" (John 14:26) The Holy Spirit is available to help us in our lives!

# THE CHALLENGE

Go to your Heavenly Father and ask Him to send the Holy Spirit. Don't go through this life without your Divine Helper.

## DAY 11 | RIGHT NOW HELP

\* \* \*

"God is our refuge and strength, A very present help in trouble." (Psalm 46:1)

In today's Challenge, let's start with some reflection questions:

- Who do we go to first when we are in trouble? Who do we go to when you need help?

- Do you fully understand that the Lord wants you to go to Him when we need Him?

The Lord wants to help you! Yes, He does. God is available to help you! He is our right now help!

In the previous challenge, we proclaimed God as the real source of our strength and our help. The Holy Spirit is our advocate, our guide, and our helper. He is always there, loving us, ready to lead and guide us. Again, The **Holy Spirit** is our **compass** (the divine instrument pointing us in the right direction). The **Word of God** is our roadmap (the detailed guide of the path to our destination). [See the Day 2 Challenge]. Our relationship with the Lord shouldn't be limited to us crying out to him for help, but it is comforting to know that He is with us when we need him!

# *THE CHALLENGE*

Go to God first! Let Him not be our last option! Don't be ashamed to cry out to Him in your time of need. Make up in your mind that God will NOT be your last option

# DAY 12 | OUR SAFE PLACE

\* \* \*

## "God is our refuge and strength, A very present help in trouble." (Psalm 46:1)

The word *refuge* is used multiple times in the Old Testament and the Psalms. David was on the run from King Saul. Saul sought to kill David because he was jealous of David's anointing on his life. When David was on the run, he had to seek a place of *"refuge"* or **a place where he would be safe from danger from the enemy who was after him.** It is expressed in this text that the **Lord is our refuge.** In other words, the Lord is **our protection, our shelter, and our covering. God is our safe place!**

As men, we don't like to be in a place where we are vulnerable or weak. However, we need to admit that we need God to be our protection and our covering. We need God to protect our minds, our body, our heart, and our spirit. We need to run to Him for refuge daily! Men, we can have a safe place in the presence of God. God is our refuge!

# THE CHALLENGE

Ask God to protect us. Our minds, our emotions, our destinies need the covering of the Lord! Starting today, pray daily for the Lord to be your refuge.

## DAY 13 | LIGHT ALWAYS WINS!

\* \* \*

**The LORD is my light and my salvation—so why should I be afraid? The LORD is my fortress, protecting me from danger, so why should I tremble? (Psalm 27:1 NLT)**

**Light is more powerful than darkness.**

Wherever light goes, darkness flees. The night is no longer night when the sun comes up. This is the power of light. Good Man, mighty warrior, you don't have to live in darkness. Jesus told His disciples, *"I am the light of the world. Whoever follows me will not walk in darkness but will have the light of life." (John 8:12)* Jesus is indeed the LIGHT of the world! He wants to be your light that shines bright. John's Gospel also states, *"In him was life, and that life was the light of all mankind. The light shines in the darkness, and the darkness has not overcome it."* Light always wins!

The psalmist proclaims in the text that *"The LORD is my light...so why be afraid?"* His light **illuminates** truth. His light shines bright in your moments of darkness. His light exposes the dangers that are lurking and seeking to overtake the believer. His light brings warmth when the world is cold. His light makes life bright! **Light always wins!**

# *THE CHALLENGE*

Let His Light shine in your life! Do not live in darkness! Ask God for His Light to shine on you.

# DAY 14 | LOVE YOUR WIFE

\* \* \*

**Husbands, love your wives, just as Christ also loved the church and gave Himself up for her. (Ephesians 5:25 NIV)**

The Word of God says, "*Marriage is honorable among all, and the bed undefiled; but fornicators and adulterers God will judge." (Hebrews 13:4)* These next couple of challenges will deal with marriage and family.

Husbands, love your wives! Isn't this what husbands are supposed to do? Why did the Apostle Paul include this statement in his letter to the church in Ephesus? Paul was dealing with sexual immorality and other issues, which was the norm in this culture. These are some of the same problems we are dealing with today. The Apostle Paul taught this local church how to turn away from ungodly lifestyles and behaviors and embrace their new life in Christ.

During those times, damages were done to the family structure because of the culture of sexual immorality and other sin issues. Husbands were unfaithful to their wives. They didn't know how to honor and respect women as a whole because they were just sexual objects to them. Women were viewed as property. This behavior was the norm. Generation after generation taught this social norm to their sons. The Apostle Paul taught the church how marriage and family should be. He taught husbands how God expected them to treat their wives.

**Jesus Christ, Himself** set the standard of how to love our wives! The church is the bride of Christ. Christ gave his all to the church on the cross. He died so that the church can live. Husbands, Christ set the standard for loving our wives by His example of how he loved the church.

If you are dating, plan on dating, or praying for a future wife, prepare and seek God as you get ready for your future wife. If you are divorced and want to remarry, don't let the previous marriage define you. Be the GOOD MAN God has called you to be. Don't let your past marriage ruin your future one. Let's be good husbands. Let's strive to be a GOOD MAN.

# *THE CHALLENGE*

Love your wife! Examine how you are treating and loving her. The standard that the Word gave us for loving our wives is so high that we can't do it in our own strength. Our daily prayer should be to ask God to help us treat our wives better and to love our wives deeper. God will teach us how to love our wives if we let Him.

## DAY 15 | HOW DEEP IS YOUR LOVE?

\* \* \*

*Husbands, love your wives, just as Christ also loved the church and gave Himself up for her. (Ephesians 5:25 NIV)*

How deep is the love for your wife? Is it as deep as the love Christ has for the church? We aim to love our wives as deeply as Christ has shown for His Love for the church.

One may ask, "What if she doesn't love me that way?" "What if she does me wrong?" "What if I'm doing all of the work?" A good relationship is not one-sided. Imagine how Jesus feels? We are the church. We are God's Creation. We didn't love Him as much as He loved us. We all have done God wrong. Jesus did all of the work on the cross. He has been faithful to us when we were not faithful to Him!

How we treat our wives is a reflection of how we treat the Lord Himself. Your wife is God's daughter. She is God's gift to you. We are to treat our wives like the gifts that they are. Paul was teaching the Ephesian church devotion to their wives. The same lessons still apply because your wife is your gift!

# *THE CHALLENGE*

Think about God's grace, mercy, and forgiveness. Think about the love God has shown you, despite mistakes and flaws. Strive to love your wife just like that!

# DAY 16 | COVER WITH LOVE

\* \* \*

> "Above all, keep fervent in your love for one another, because love covers a multitude of sins." (1 Peter 4:8 NASB)

**We are on Day 16,** and we are about halfway through. I trust that these challenges are blessing you. We are about to go deeper. Here we go!

In **1 Peter 4:8**, the Apostle Peter expresses how God's love through Jesus' sacrifice on the cross covers our past sins when we are converted to believers. This text is often misquoted because some use this scripture to justify sin and ungodly lifestyles. When you read the entire chapter in its context, Peter encourages the church to live according to the will of God.

Our love for others is a reflection of our love for Christ Himself! Our love for others is an extension of the love of God. This love is not just talking but action. Just like God didn't throw us away or stop loving us, we shouldn't be quick to throw others away. The Word love used in this text come from the phrase **(agápē) ἀγάπη,** which means *"divine love,"* the love of God, or love that comes from God Himself!

This type of love is either shown to us by God or the expressed love towards others by God. This love is not by our own power. Learn to cover someone else with love!

# THE CHALLENGE

Start to love others with agape love! Ask God today to put His Love in your heart towards others. He loves us, and it is His will that we (the church) be the extension of God's Love toward others.

# DAY 17 | LOVE HAS POWER

\* \* \*

**"Most important of all, continue to show deep love for each other, for love covers a multitude of sins." (1 Peter 4:6 NLT)**

*"How can we love others when we feel they do us wrong?"*

*"I don't want to be weak!"*

*"I'm not going to be anyone's pushover!"*

These are some of the things other men have said in men's bible study or men's group. Growing up in Detroit, I was taught not to be weak! "Be tough!" "Don't show weakness!" Some defined this as manhood. Honestly, most of us men have not been adequately taught the power of love. As corny as it may sound, **love does have power!**

As we covered in the last Challenge, the Apostle Peter in **1 Peter 4:6** was expressing how the love of God through Jesus' sacrifice on the Cross covers our past sins. The Apostle also says that we should show deep love to others as Jesus revealed to us. Look at how powerful God's love is! We should show love like Jesus.

Let today be a starting point; this is not an overnight process. If you sincerely ask God, He will make some changes on the inside of you. But, there are things you will have to do also. You will have to forgive, let things go, trust people, express love, and change other behaviors. Your marriage or relationship, family, children, loved ones, and the community will be better because you are deciding to love!

The **GOOD MAN** journey is not an easy one, but it is a life-changing one! Love has power!

# THE CHALLENGE

Right now, decide to love! Period. Ask God now to put love in your heart.

# DAY 18 | FALL IN LOVE WITH JESUS, AGAIN!

\* \* \*

**"But I have this complaint against you. You don't love me or each other as you did at first!" (Revelation 2:4 NLT)**

Do you remember your first true love? Whether it was a person, hobby, or anything else. That young lady was on your mind all the time. You wanted to be around them all of the time. If it was a hobby or activity, you wanted to be engaged in it. We are not talking about lust; we are talking about true love. Some men will say they never experienced true love. I disagree with that statement. I believe we all have loved something or someone in this life.

In some romantic relationships, break-ups happen. The point is either your heart was broken, or you broke their heart. If you ever had your heartbroken from someone leaving you, it is a terrible feeling.

In **Revelations,** John writes about seven churches. One of the churches he writes about is the church in Ephesus. He compliments the church on their endurance and good works. But he also says, *"... I have this against you, that you have abandoned the love you had at first."*

Notice the Church in Ephesus was doing good works, but the "good works" itself didn't equal love. As men, many of us were taught if we "do things," it equals love. Love shows action, but love is more than the effort we offer. Love is also about what is in our hearts. We should ask ourselves, "Is my heart in what I do?" John is saying that the Church in Ephesus' heart wasn't in what they did. They were "going through the motions."

In your meaningful relationships, are you just "going through the motions?" I have been guilty myself. Most importantly, are you just "going through the motions" with God? Brothers, let's get that part right! If we get that part right with God, we will see other areas of our lives changed.

**Let's fall in love with GOD again!**

# *THE CHALLENGE*

Let's fall in love with GOD. Either for the first time or again. Commit to having a more profound love for God!

# DAY 19 | TURN AROUND

\* \* \*

**"But I have this against you, that you have abandoned the love you had at first. Remember therefore from where you have fallen; repent and do the works you did at first. If not, I will come to you and remove your lampstand from its place, unless you repent." (Revelation 2:4-5 NLT)**

**Ready to go further? Let's do this!**

On Day 19, we will continue with the book of Revelation chapter 2, verse 4, and we will add verse 5. Verse 4 talks about the church in Ephesus, leaving their "first love" (Jesus Christ). Verse 5 takes this even further where John is expressing coming back to that same love. "Remember therefore from where you have fallen; repent..."

Let's look at this Word: **repent.**

**Repent, metanoeó μετανοέω** *(met-an-o-eh'-o)* means to change or turn one's mind or purpose. It also means to turn completely around. To turn one direction and go the opposite way. A 180° degree turn. John was saying to the church of Ephesus that their hearts turned toward God at one time, but their heart turned away at some time. In verse 5, The Apostle tells the church to turn your heart back toward Jesus. That is the same message to us today, brothers.

The beginning of our relationship with God starts with repentance. *"If you confess with your mouth that Jesus is Lord and believe in your heart that God raised him from the dead, you will be saved. For with the heart, one believes and is justified, and with the mouth, one confesses and is saved." (Romans 10:9-10)* Believing (or turning) of your heart is what happens inwardly as you confess with your mouth or verbally speak aloud that Jesus is Lord. Not only will your heart turn around, but your will life also turns around. Repentance should not be a one-time event, but it is a daily experience. Every day, brothers, we should repent and make sure that our hearts are turned to Jesus, our true love.

**37**

# *THE CHALLENGE*

Starting today, make a daily habit of repenting. These are not just words, but your heart must turn. A changed heart will change behavior. Your life will continue to change. Turn around.

## DAY 20 | RESPECT

\* \* \*

"**The fear of the LORD is the beginning of knowledge; Fools despise wisdom and instruction.**" (Proverbs 1:7 NLT)

Brothers, our relationship with the Lord should be the top priority in our life. We must seek God daily and grow in our faith. This scripture expresses that *"The fear of the LORD is the beginning of knowledge."* The word *"fear"* is not talking about being afraid, but this Word fear means *"reverence."* The definition of reverence is a deep respect for someone or something; to honor, have high esteem, and have a great admiration.

To have reverence and honor of God is the beginning of knowledge. By honoring God, He reveals Himself to us and gives revelation to things about life. He gives us wisdom and guides our path. It is good to know the Lord! There are benefits to having a personal relationship with the Lord.

# *THE CHALLENGE*

Give reverence and honor to God. Seek to know God better. You will find that you will begin to gain more knowledge.

# DAY 21 | CHILDREN ARE A REWARD

\* \* \*

**"Behold, children are a heritage from the Lord, the fruit of the womb a reward." (Psalm 127:3 NASB)**

In my opinion, man's most incredible gifts are children. Children are full of potential and promise. However, guidance is needed for that potential to be realized and utilized. There are some wonderful fathers out there that are doing the best that they can for their children. Unfortunately, many children of our day are living in a fatherless home. It is a stereotype among men of color that they will grow up without a father raising them. According to the 2019 U.S. Census Bureau, 4 out of 11 million single-parent families with children under 18 and single mothers headed 80 percent. This is across ethnic lines. There are many reasons why there are single-mother homes. However, that does not erase the fact that our sons and daughters need us (fathers) in their lives.

In biblical times, a man's wealth was in how many children he had. Generational blessings and identity were a substantial part of Hebrew culture. The Father was a vital figure in the household. Fathers were responsible for teaching their sons the ways of life, the law, their family heritage, etc. The identity of the family came from the father.

**Brothers, your children need you, your family needs you, and your community needs you!** The next generation requires your strength, your presence, your gifts, and your guidance. We don't know what all the next generation will produce, but they need our help to build it! Our children are a reward!

# *THE CHALLENGE*

Embrace your children. Give them your time, encouragement, support, love, listening ear, guidance, and whatever is needed for them to achieve greatness!

## DAY 22 | PROVOKE NOT

\* \* \*

"Behold, children are a heritage from the Lord, the fruit of the womb a reward." (Psalm 127:3 NASB)

**Father, Grandfather, Stepfather, Uncle, Great-Uncle, Mentor, Elder, Minister, Pastor,** you have a role to play in a younger person's life. It is possible to be present but still missing. Trust me; I get it: I'm a father, uncle, big brother, and pastor. I have natural and spiritual sons. I'm swamped and sometimes overwhelmed. Fathers all over the world understand how I feel. I'm finding out that what my sons want the most is **my time.** What they need the most is **my guidance.**

You have something to give to your children and the next generation that cannot be replaced: **YOU! You are irreplaceable.** You have something to give the next generation. Even with all the mistakes we made, we can share how not to make the same mistakes with the next generation. Your experience is more valuable than your money. Let's reach the next generation and show them the right way!

# *THE CHALLENGE*

Think about who you can pour into. Ask God for more wisdom. Of course, pour into your own seed, but who else can gain from your experience and guidance? If your relationship with your children is broken, ask God to fix it. If the connection is beyond repair, ask God to lead you to someone who can guide you. You have something to offer!

## DAY 23 | HANDLE WITH CARE

\* \* \*

"Fathers, do not provoke your children to anger by the way you treat them. Rather, bring them up with the discipline and instruction that comes from the Lord." (Ephesians 6:4 NLT)

**Father or Father-figures:** How we treat people matters, especially our children. The way we treat our kids can make or break them. If we are not careful, we (fathers) can cause trauma and pain. Inadequate treatment can cause damage. Some men and women are suffering from emotional trauma because of their fathers' maltreatment. You may be reading this book and suffering from your father's actions—physical, verbal, and emotional abuse from your childhood. If that applies to you, **In the name of Jesus: BE HEALED!**

The Apostle Paul wrote in the letter to the Ephesian church a warning to fathers: *do not provoke your children to anger by the way you treat them.* Instead, bring them up with the discipline and instruction that comes from the Lord. If you are reading this and you are a father or father-figure, know that God can give you how to share property discipline and instruct your children. We (fathers) can shape them or break them. **Handle with care!**

# *THE CHALLENGE*

Today's Challenge is simple, love on your children. Someone may say, "I already love on my children." Maybe you do, but today, **really love on your children**. Call them, see how their day is going, take a minute to do something special for them today. Give them your full attention today! You will be blessed!

## DAY 24 | EMBRACE GRACE

\* \* \*

**"For it is by grace you have been saved, through faith and this is not from yourselves, it is the gift of God not by works so that no one can boast." (Ephesians 2:8-9 KJV)**

Grace is mighty.

**Grace** is the *"free and unmerited favor of God."* Grace is not earned; it is given. We are saved by grace. It is the extension of the love of Jesus toward us.

Because the grace of God was given freely to us through Jesus' sacrifice on the cross, the grace of God shouldn't be taken for granted. Apostle Paul was expressing this truth to the church in Rome. Individuals in the church still wanted to live the same ungodly lifestyles they lived before they became believers. Paul reminded the church about the grace of God and that the true believer is dead to sin. The true believer should not continue to live a life of sin, period. We should never take advantage of God's grace. **Embrace Grace!**

# *THE CHALLENGE*

Do not continue in sin! We can (through Christ and the power of the Holy Spirit) live a life free from sin. Embrace His grace!

# DAY 25 | YOU DON'T HAVE TO WORK FOR IT

\* \* \*

**"For it is by grace you have been saved, through faith and this is not from yourselves, it is the gift of God not by works so that no one can boast." (Ephesians 2:8-9)**

Let's continue on the subject of grace! Again, we are saved by grace. Grace is a precious gift from God Himself. Anything we do for God should come from a place of love, honor, and respect. As men, we are used to working for something. We don't have to work for God's love. He loves you, period—**The End.**

The work of redemption through Jesus Christ is because of **His love** for us. You don't have to work for it. You don't have to "punch in a time clock" to earn it. We work on our jobs, businesses, education, and even church. Ministry is sometimes hard work, but God gives us the grace for the work of ministry. **We don't have to work for God's grace!** Thank God for grace!

# *THE CHALLENGE*

Today is a simple challenge. Thank God right now for grace!

# DAY 26 | LIVE FREE!

\* \* \*

**"For God saved us and called us to live a holy life. He did this, not because we deserved it, but because that was his plan from before the beginning of time—to show us his grace through Christ Jesus." (2 Timothy 1:9)**

We are going further in this subject of **grace**. We don't deserve grace because we did nothing to earn it. Again, the work of redemption through Jesus Christ is because of His love. Every believer who has accepted Jesus in their heart as Lord and Savior are living off of grace. We don't work for it, but that doesn't mean we don't do anything as believers.

Timothy writes, *"For God saved us and called us to live a holy life."* Brothers, you are called by God, called to live a different life than you were living while you were a sinner. Remember, no one can earn God's favor; it is a gift because we belong to God. We live a holy life because we are now changed inside and out. Don't be a prisoner! Sin keeps us in prison, but Jesus died to free us. When you are born-again (accepting Jesus into your heart), you receive your pardon. Maintain your freedom. **Live Free!**

# THE CHALLENGE

Embrace your salvation! Flee from sin. Live for God by asking for His help to avoid all the pitfalls of sin.

# DAY 27 | LIVE HOLY!

\* \* \*

**"For God saved us and called us to live a holy life."**
**(2 Timothy 1:9)**

Brothers, the word *Holy* can be intimidating. Our theological and church circles, living a holy life, have different meanings to different people. Let's examine this Word: Holy (*hagios*) ἅγος: "*set apart by (or for) a sacred purpose, likeness of nature with the Lord, and different from the world.*" This is a biblical truth that all born-again believers around the world should embrace. Brothers, we are called to be different from the world. Lying, cheating, stealing, and other behaviors should not be a part of the believer's life. *"For God saved us and called us to live a holy life."*

Someone may say:

"I'm not perfect!"
"That is impossible."
"No one can live without sinning."
"We all make mistakes."

If we depend on our strength alone, that is true. One of the Holy Spirit's functions is to live inside us and keep us from falling back into sin. Again, **The Holy Spirit** is our *compass (the divine instrument pointing us in the right direction)*, and the **Word of God** is our **roadmap** (*the detailed guide of the path to our destination*). We are called to live a holy life. **Live Holy!**

# *THE CHALLENGE*

The Challenge is to ask God to fill you with His Spirit to help you to live holy. If you are already filled with His Spirit, ask for a refilling. "Lord, fill me with your Holy Spirit!"

# DAY 28 | GET POWER

\* \* \*

**"But you will receive power when the Holy Spirit comes upon you. And you will be my witnesses, telling people about me everywhere-in Jerusalem, throughout Judea, in Samaria, and to the ends of the earth." (Acts" 1:8)**

### POWER.

Most of us crave some type of power. It may be financial, political, physical, or other forms of power. I have good news for you! Power is available to you without stepping over anyone, cheating anyone, paying for it, and so forth. Once you get it, your life will be better for it!

In the **first chapter of Acts**, Jesus was having His last earthly conversion with His followers before He ascends to heaven. The disciples kept asking him, *"Lord, "as the time come for you to free Israel and restore our kingdom?" (Acts"1:6)* The disciples were concern about the politics of that time and wanted to know when Jesus was going to take over Israel.

Jesus replied, *"The Father alone has the authority to set those dates and times, and they are not for you to know. But you will receive power when the Holy Spirit comes upon you. And you will be my witnesses, telling people about me everywhere-in Jerusalem, throughout Judea, in Samaria, and to the ends of the earth."* Jesus" commands His followers to go to Jerusalem to get POWER because He had kingdom work for them to do. This same **POWER (*dunamis*: dynamic power, force, or ability)** is available for every believer. Seek it, desire it! Walk in the power of the Lord!

# *THE CHALLENGE*

The Challenge today is to seek **THE POWER OF THE HOLY SPIRIT!** If you have experienced the baptism of the Holy Spirit before, continue to seek more power. His power is limitless.

# DAY 29 | STRONG WIND

\* \* \*

"On the day of Pentecost, all the believers were meeting together in one place. Suddenly, there was a sound from heaven like the roaring of a mighty windstorm, and it filled the house where they were sitting. Then, what looked like flames or tongues of fire appeared and settled on each of them. And everyone present was filled with the Holy Spirit and began speaking in other languages, as the Holy Spirit gave them this ability." (Acts 2:1-4 NLT)

**National Geographic** states on its website that "wind is the movement of air from an area of high pressure to an area of low pressure. Wind exists because the sun unevenly heats the surface of the Earth. As hot air rises, cooler air moves in to fill the void. As long as the sun shines, the wind will blow. And the wind has long served as a power source to humans." Look at the statement, "As long " as the sun shines, the wind will blow." That can be a spiritual statement as well, for as long as the **Son (Jesus)** shines, **the wind (The Holy Spirit)** will blow **(send His Power)!**

The bible records in Acts 2:1-4 that the New Testament church gathered together in Jerusalem in an upper room, following a commandment from Jesus to wait from the Greek Word orπμ or *perimenó περιμένω (per-ee-men'-o)* in **Acts, chapter 1.** Jesus told them to **wait** *(remain, abide, be steady regardless of the obstacles involved, endure by putting up with difficulty, be patient, wait by serving.)* Jesus promised that they *"will receive power when the Holy Spirit has come upon you." (Acts" 1:8).* That was what happened in *Acts 2, "When the day of Pentecost arrived, they were all together in one place. And suddenly there came from heaven a sound like a mighty rushing wind, and it filled the entire house where they were sitting."* The promise was fulfilled, and they received the power of the Holy Spirit. This **DUNAMIS POWER** *(dynamic power,* *force, or ability)* is available for every believer. Most of all, this power is available for you! **Strong winds are blowing!**

# *THE CHALLENGE*

Be determined to walk in the Power of the Holy Spirit. Let the Holy Spirit be a part of your daily walk.

# DAY 30 | CATCH ON FIRE

\* \* \*

"On the day of Pentecost, all the believers were meeting together in one place. Suddenly, there was a sound from heaven like the roaring of a mighty windstorm, and it filled the house where they were sitting. Then, what looked like flames or tongues of fire appeared and settled on each of them. And everyone present was filled with the Holy Spirit and began speaking in other languages, as the Holy Spirit gave them this ability." (Acts 2:1-4 NLT)

**Fire** is the visible effect of the process of combustion – a particular type of chemical reaction. It occurs between oxygen in the air and some kind of fuel. Combustion occurs when fuel heats to its ignition temperature. The response will keep going as long as there are enough heat, fuel, and oxygen. This is known as the fire triangle.

Combustion is when fuel reacts with oxygen that releases both heat and light. Combustion can be slow or fast, depending on the amount of oxygen available. As long as there are enough fuel and oxygen, the fire will keep burning.

In the Bible, fire also represents several things:

- The guiding presence of God among His people.
- God's holiness and protection over his people.
- A purifying agent in the life of the believer.

This is what the Holy Spirit will do when He is operating in the life of the believer. The Holy Spirit will: **guide, give power, and purify.** In the previous Challenge, we talked about the power of the wind, but God also wants to provide you with the power of fire! Catch on Fire!

**Act 2:3** declares that *"there appeared unto them (the church) cloven tongues like as of fire, and it sat upon each of them."* God wanted the first-century church to have the power of wind and fire (spiritually). As the church did what they were called to do (change the world), He wanted them to be filled with the Holy Spirit to empower them to accomplish their mission. Again, that same power is available for you right now. It is vital, brothers, to have **the fire** (The Holy Spirit) to be the mighty warrior, the GOOD MAN that God calls us to be.

It's a promise from God, the Father. **Seek and desire the power of fire!**

# THE CHALLENGE

Catch on fire and stay on fire! This fire is needed to be all God wants us to be. This fire will guide, give power, and purify us.

# CONCLUSION

**CONGRATULATIONS!** You finished the Challenge. How do you feel? This is the end of this book, but not the end of the journey. The journey continues for a lifetime. Continue to grow as a: son, brother, husband, father, mentor, and MAN.

The last Challenge for you is to share the Gospel of Jesus Christ with someone else. Tell someone else about the goodness of the Lord. Tell another person how God changed your life.

The PRAYER OF REPENTANCE AND DEDICATION (on the next page) was in the Day One Challenge. As you evangelize others, use the prayer on the next page to win others to Jesus Christ. After sharing the Gospel with your testimony, ask the person to repeat this prayer with you. If you are leading a small group or teaching a Bible study, ask your group, "Does anyone want to know Jesus as their Lord and Savior?" then ask everyone to repeat the prayer on the next page.

# A PRAYER OF REPENTANCE AND DEDICATION

The Bible tells us in **Romans 10:9 (NIV),** *"If you declare with your mouth, Jesus is Lord," and believe in your heart that God raised him from the dead, you will be saved.* For it is with your heart that you believe and is justified, and it is with your mouth that you profess your faith and are saved." Verse 13 goes on to say, *"Whosoever calls on the name of the Lord shall be saved."* "Whosoever" means you and me! For Repentance and Dedication, repeat this prayer out loud:

"Dear J" sus, I want you to guide my life. You said in Your Word that if I acknowledge that You were raised from the dead and that I accept you as my Lord and Savior, I would be saved. So, God, I now say that I believe You are MY RISEN SAVIOR, and I want you now to be Lord over my life! I accept my salvation from sin right now.

After the prayer, let the person or the group know that God has forgiven them and that they are a new creation! This has been an incredible journey. Now go and change the world!

## CONNECT WITH THE AUTHOR

## Keith Martin

Visit the website: www.keith-martin.com

Facebook @keith.martin.jr

Twitter: @keith_martinjr

Instagram: @keith_martinjr

Made in the USA
Monee, IL
29 March 2021